TEDDY ALVA

BURNOUT

The Essential Guide on How to Handle Burnout, Learn The Proven Strategies and Useful Tips on How You Can Recognize, Prevent and Overcome Burnout

Descrierea CIP a Bibliotecii Naționale a României
TEDDY ALVA
BURNOUT. The Essential Guide on How to Handle Burnout, Learn The Proven Strategies and Useful Tips on How You Can Recognize, Prevent and Overcome Burnout / Teddy Alva – Bucharest: Editura My Ebook, 2021
ISBN

TEDDY ALVA

BURNOUT

The Essential Guide on How to Handle Burnout, Learn The Proven Strategies and Useful Tips on How You Can Recognize, Prevent and Overcome Burnout

My Ebook Publishing House
Bucharest, 2021

TABLE OF CONTENTS

Introduction	7
Spotting Burnout	13
Preventing Burnout	17
Energy Management	18
Outsourcing	20
Decision Fatigue	22
Make Sacrifices	23
Habits and Lifestyle	24
Learning to Relax	27
Cognitive Behavioral Therapy	31
Nutrition, Exercise and Sleep	35
Recovering From Burnout	40
How to Recover From Burnout	41
Conclusion	45

INTRODUCTION

All of us want to do more and it's all too common to feel as though there aren't enough hours in the day. Unfortunately though, our energy is finite and when we push too far or too fast we will inevitably burn out and have to give up.

This is not only very upsetting because it means we aren't able to do everything we would like to – it's also a very unpleasant feeling that leaves us drained, exhausted and prone to illness. What's worse, we tend to become moody, we lose all interest in the things that normally switch us on and we generally become shadows of our former selves.

And even when you *aren't* trying so hard to push past your limits and 'fit everything in' it's still all-too easy to reach burnout. Our modern lifestyle it seems is just jam packed with things to do and places to be. If you're not rushing around and staying late at work, you're travelling home on a busy and crowded commute or you're tidying the house, responding to e-mails and juggling your social life and family responsibilities. Is it any wonder that so many of us feel fit to explode?

Many of us will even know that we're working towards burnout and feel almost completely powerless to stop it. We can *feel* the cold developing in the back of our throat, our eyes are starting to feel heavy and we would do anything just to get ten minutes to sit down and read a book with a cup of tea…

We often know when burnout is on the way but unfortunately it tends to be somewhat inevitable. And what follows is days or weeks of low energy, bad moods and illness. Burnout can even cause bad skin, impotence and low libido, weight gain or loss and accidents. It's no laughing matter.

Sometimes we'll even work *through* the burnout – never quite recovering, never quite doing our best work and never really enjoying anything that life has to offer. In fact, there's a good chance that's how you feel right now and that you're just *perpetually* burned out.

What is Burnout?

But what is burnout really? Sure – it's that feeling of being tired, achy and stressed and an inability to perform. And *sure* it stands to reason that we can't keep pushing ourselves without collapsing eventually.

But why not? If you're getting enough food and enough sleep for energy, then why *can't* you just keep going?

The main problem is chronic stress. When you're working hard to try and stay productive, you will experience chronic stress. In itself that's not even necessarily a bad thing. Stress is simply motivation that is born out of your neurotransmitters. When you believe that things need to be done and that something deserves your attention, your body treats it the same way it would treat a physical threat – by flooding your brain and body with dopamine, norepinephrine and adrenaline. This little cocktail encourages focus, memory, alertness and more.

And it's actually a *good* thing. Stress as a motivator is called 'eustress' and without it most of us would never get off of the couch.

The problem is when it just keeps going and going and you never get any respite. You see, while stress hormones make you faster, stronger and more engaged they also suppress your immune system and your digestion - sending blood and energy to more deserving functions in your body for the tasks at hand. If this continues you will stand to get ill – even if you're getting enough sleep and vitamins.

Then there's the fact that stress hormones increase your blood pressure and your heartrate. Blood viscosity increases in the presence of adrenaline so that you will bleed less if you get injured. Again, that sounds useful but in the long term it's not healthy and it can even put you at risk of heart attack.

There are psychological implications too. Simply knowing that you have work piled up and back-to-back appointments for the next year is enough to drive anyone a little mad. It leaves you with nothing to look forward too and it should be no surprise that this can cause you to get upset. Worst case scenario, this can lead to what psychologists call 'learned helplessness'.

Basically this means that you've 'trained' yourself to believe that there's no way out and that the work will just keep coming. The solution? Give up. At least that way you preserve energy.

When you're working non-stop you're also *not* doing all the other things you should be doing. The house isn't getting tidied, you're not spending time with friends and you're probably burning the candle at both ends. You might even be eating more takeout meals instead of cooking things that are healthy and nourishing.

But the *real* problems start once you get to 'adrenal fatigue'. Adrenal fatigue means that the continuous production of adrenaline and other stress hormones has worn out your adrenal glands. This then means your body will be unable to produce more of the chemicals that keep you motivated and focused. You *literally* run out juice. You *burn out*.

What to do About Burnout?

The question then, is whether burn-out can be prevented. Can you still get everything done that you want to do? Can you still fit in all those appointments? And can you do this *without* collapsing? How do you get control back and start feeling like you're *on top* of things again?

Furthermore, what do you do about it once it happens? How do you get that energy and drive *back* afterwards? That's what we'll be looking at in the next few chapters. Keep reading and you'll be able to say goodbye to burnout once and for all by fueling your body with energy and power and by managing your time and energy far more effectively.

SPOTTING BURNOUT

Spotting burnout isn't always easy, especially when you're so rushed and stressed that you barely have time to pet the dog before you rush out the door without your keys.

But learning to spot burnout is the first crucial step in getting a handle on it. You can't fight what you can't see – so if you don't learn to identify the warning signs when they first emerge you'll be falling at the first hurdle every time.

Signs You Might be Experiencing Burnout

Here are some of the signs that you might be experiencing psychological and physical burnout…

- You find it difficult to wake up in the morning
- You find it difficult to get to sleep

- If you work out, you might notice symptoms of overtraining such as lethargy and achy joints that make it hard to train
  - Aches and pains become more prominent
  - Irritability
  - You find it hard to concentrate
  - You procrastinate more than normal, often spending hours surfing the web or playing mobile games
  - You lose enthusiasm for things that would normally excite you
  - Reduced sex drive
  - Impotence
  - Loss of appetite
  - Weight loss
  - Weight gain
  - You make lots of small mistakes that you normally wouldn't, possibly resulting in accidents
  - You fall asleep at unsuitable times/in unsuitable places
  - Headaches
  - Depression

- Lack of creativity/new ideas
- Writers' block
- Susceptibility to colds and flus
- Bad skin
- Tinnitus (ringing in the ears)
- IBS
- Indigestion

No one person will experience all the same symptoms and you won't necessarily find that all of the above apply in your particular case. However, it's nevertheless true that these are some of the biggest signs of burnout and some of the things you are most likely to notice if you are experiencing it.

One of the best terms that is often used to describe essentially what it feels like to be burned out is 'tired but wired'. In other words, you will feel exhausted but at the same time kind of wired. The point to remember is that although your adrenaline has burned out, the causes of stress and the motivating factors are still there – so you still have the increased cortisol and dopamine which will make it hard for you to 'switch off' properly. This is why your thoughts will race and you'll find it difficult to relax, sleep and recover and it's why you'll find you only get worse until you do something about it.

As you know, prevention is better than a cure. That is to say that if you can notice any of these symptoms early – even if it's just one or two of these things – you should consider it as a warning sign of potentially impending burnout. Don't wait for all the symptoms to be present: act right away!

PREVENTING BURNOUT

Now you know the symptoms and signs associated with burnout and what it is, you may have a better chance of identifying it as it starts to occur. This means that you can take action but that's where the next challenge arises. Just precisely what can you do to get things back under your control and to aid your body in handling the burnout?

Read on and let's take a look at some of the best options you have available to you…

ENERGY MANAGEMENT

Any productivity guru or business management expert you talk to is likely to go on and on about time management. Time management means thinking carefully about how you can make the best and most efficient use of your time in order to fit everything in. You might use scheduling software, a smart diary system or any other manner of tools in order to better arrange your time so you can get more done and in an ideal world – also have more time to spend with your family etc.

The problem with time management though is that it leaves out a rather important additional factor: your energy.

Simply ask yourself this: just because you can fit X amount of appointments in, do you think that this means you *should*? If you had unlimited energy reserves and willpower and no other commitments in your life then maybe the answer would be yes but as you're no doubt aware – that's just not the case.

Think about what you do most evenings. Do you use your time productively? Or is there at least an hour or two that you spend completely collapsed on the couch?

If you answered the latter, then you might be thinking 'great, that means I can make phone calls/do a workout/take up Pilates.

But then you should ask yourself another question: if it were that easy, then don't you think you'd be doing something useful with that time *already*?

That's where energy management comes in and it's where you need to think about your energy reserves as a finite resource just like time. Limit yourself to doing five 'productive things' a day and then recognize that anything further you do is going to result in diminishing returns.

And what's more, you should also acknowledge the need for resting and recharging. In other words, you should schedule in an opportunity to recharge your batteries as though it were a crucial appointment that couldn't be missed. Every single day should have at least one block of 'you time'.

Apart from preventing burnout this is just also how you keep life enjoyable, rewarding and fulfilling. If you're constantly doing things you don't want to, then what are you even doing?

OUTSOURCING

Now you might be thinking 'but I don't have *time* to schedule in me time'! When you're so busy that you're driving yourself to the point of burnout, it's much easier said than done to just 'take some time out'. Taking time out means you need to remove something *else* from your schedule and right now everything probably seems much too important to be removed.

One solution to this issue is to start outsourcing. In other words, find tasks that don't require you to do them personally and then give the job to someone else. Even if it costs you some money to do this, it's important to recognize the *value* of your time and why this is a smart exchange.

At work this might mean simply delegating your tasks to colleagues, staff or anyone else who can handle aspects of your workload. Alternatively it might require you to hire extra team members, or perhaps to use a virtual assistant – someone who can do a range of administrative tasks for you remotely for a very low fee (often this means outsourcing to India, so make sure the task doesn't require perfect English).

You can also outsource jobs at home though too. Perhaps your family isn't quite doing their bit and you should ask your kids or your partner to help you with more of the chores. Creating a fair itinerary for each member of the household and explaining you're struggling can often make a big difference.

Hiring a cleaner or gardener is also a very simple decision you can make that will immediately yield more time and energy for you. Or alternatively, you could use a virtual assistant to handle your home admin tasks – they can do everything from booking your holiday to organizing your 50th birthday party. And if you're planning a wedding, then using a wedding planner is worth every single cent.

DECISION FATIGUE

Don't underestimate the amount of mental energy required to make even small decisions. While it might not seem like a big deal, deciding what to have for breakfast, what to wear and where to go for dinner all take a toll on your energy levels. Making these small decisions can deplete your reserves and can end up having a cumulative effect that contributes to burnout. This is actually the reason that Steve Jobs famously wore the same black top and jeans every single day – so that he could eliminate the tiring process of having to choose what to wear. You don't have to go that far but having a consistent breakfast will make life considerably easier.

MAKE SACRIFICES

Some things can't be outsourced or automated and in these cases you might just need to make sacrifices. This is especially true if you want to start fitting something else into your schedule.

If you're planning on working out 5 hours a week consistently on top of your already hectic schedule for instance, then you're likely to find that it just doesn't work. Instead, you need to make sure that you give up something else you do regularly in order to make the time necessary for the job.

An example of this would be to give up any clubs you do regularly that you don't absolutely need. Or alternatively you might just have to say no to the occasional invitation. While it's upsetting to turn down things you want to do - or that you feel you *have* to do – ultimately it's necessary sometimes. Remember, there's a limited amount you can do. You just *can't* do everything. That means you need to prioritize.

HABITS AND LIFESTYLE

A few small changes to your lifestyle and habits can also make a big difference by giving you less stress throughout your daily routine.

One example of this is to go more minimalist and to get rid of a lot of the stuff you don't need. Most of us have boxes and rubbish on top of our wardrobes and under our beds that we never look at. You might think those boxes are harmless but in fact their mere presence will be a slight stressor when you're trying to relax in that room, they will make it more difficult to find the things you're looking for and they will get in the way if you ever need to move.

If you haven't been in one of those boxes in the last 6 months, then chances are that you don't *really* need what's in them. So bite the bullet, be ruthless and throw them out. You'll be surprised by just how liberating this is.

Likewise, if you have lots of ornaments and clutter on your surfaces you should get rid of some of that. Doing so will mean you instantly improve the average quality of what's on display (because the stuff you leave will be the best stuff) and that cleaning and tidying is 100% easier.

Try to get into good habits that will pay off in the long run. Make your bed every single morning – it's one very small step but it makes a big difference to the look of your room and it's a great way to get yourself into a productive and efficient mindset.

You should also look into investing in simple gadgets and services that can make life better. Spend all morning ironing? Get a hand-held steamer. Got piles of dirty plates in the kitchen? Get a dishwasher. Waking up with low energy in winter? Get a daylight lamp from a manufacturer like Lumie and get woken up with a natural sunrise simulation every morning. Sometimes a small purchase can make a *big* difference.

In terms of your work life meanwhile, it might be suitable to try the favored approach of Tim Ferriss (author of *The Four Hour Workweek*) who recommends using the 80/20 principle to look at the 20% of activities that deliver the 80% of results. In other words, if you have 10 clients, there's a good chance that you get the vast majority of your work from 20% of them and that the rest are just taking up a lot of your time without really paying off. The solution? Get rid of that 80% and focus on the 20% that are working for you. A lean business is more manageable and resilient and it results in a better work/life balance.

LEARNING TO RELAX

So you've made yourself some free time by cancelling plans, outsourcing things and removing a few minor decisions. This right away should make you feel a little bit better but unfortunately for many people it won't.

Why? Because although they might physically stop working and give themselves the time they need to relax, they nevertheless don't give themselves the *mental* break. If you're relaxing on the couch but you're ruminating and stressing about all the work you still have to do, then you are *not* getting the recharging break that you need. In fact it's worse in some ways because you won't have any physical tasks to distract you from your stress.

In order to properly recharge and to avoid adrenal fatigue you need to switch your *mind* off as well and you need to avoid additional sources of stressors.

If you crash in front of the TV on the couch, then you are *not* getting your batteries recharged. Instead, you're increasing cortisol levels due to the unnatural light from the TV, you're worsening aching joints by maintaining a bad posture and you're probably going to still be panicking and stressing about work while you stare at the moving images on the screen. Looking at your phone and texting is even worse. And texting *while* watching TV is pretty much an invitation for burnout.

A far *better* example of recharging your batteries would be to read a book. The reason for this is that when you read a book, you lose your inner monologue (because you're sounding out the words). This means you literally *can't* worry yourself by stressing about work and it means that you get to escape your reality for a bit. There will be less natural light, no sudden noises and you'll be able to relax much more fully. Drawing or painting is also particularly good.

Another thing you can do is to exercise. That might sound like the worst thing you can do to recharge your batteries but bear in mind that it's a *mental* break you're looking for, not necessarily a physical one.

If you're exhausted then hitting the gym isn't the best idea though as this can still create a stress response. Instead, look for gentle exercise like a stroll in the park. The natural setting will help you to relax while the light exercise will trigger the release of serotonin – a natural antidepressant/anesthetic and a perfect tonic for our stress hormones.

Yoga is also great.

Also good is to read a book in the park, to get a massage (or more) from your partner, to take a hot bath, to listen to some music, to play an instrument or to do some cooking while listening to a podcast.

In other words, you need to distract your brain, you need to stimulate the production of serotonin and you need to avoid screens. Better yet, try to choose something that you genuinely enjoy and that you can look forward to (even if that *does* mean screens). This is about the most important thing because when you do something you love doing, it will produce all the right neurochemicals.

Planning outings and events is also a good idea and keeping an element of novelty will prevent things from growing stale – just make sure that the things you do aren't too stressful in terms of getting there or socially.

Individual differences play a big role here too: some people find time around other people recharging and energizing (extroverts) while others need more private time to function optimally (introverts).

Now make sure that this is happening for at least an *hour a day*.

COGNITIVE BEHAVIORAL THERAPY

But what if you still *can't* switch off? What if you have to keep rereading lines in your book because you're worried about your day ahead? What if you've read all this so far and thought 'nah, no time!'

In that case you have gotten yourself into some unfortunate habits and you'll need to find a way to get yourself out of those.

One way to do this is with cognitive behavioral therapy. Cognitive behavioral therapy is a psychotherapeutic technique used by psychologists to help people combat all kinds of bad habits that play a role in depression, anxiety, phobias and more.

The idea is to try and 'reprogram' your thought process in order to encourage positive behaviors and emotions. So in the case of agoraphobia (fear of open spaces) you would first identify the negative thoughts causing you to feel scared such as 'everyone is staring at me' (this process is called 'mindfulness'), then you would work to try and replace those thought patterns (cognitive restructuring) by challenging your current beliefs (thought challenging) and testing the ideas to see if they're true (hypothesis testing).

How might we apply this to the sense of perpetual urgency and stress that leads to burnout? The process would likely look like this:

Mindfulness: Next time you can't switch off or you feel like you need to keep working, make a note of the actual thought processes that are leading to this behavior. What is it that you are literally thinking to prevent yourself from being 'allowed' to relax. It might be something like 'I must send that e-mail before tomorrow', or 'my client will leave me if I don't upload that work', or 'I need to call my friend or they'll be so offended they'll never speak to me again'.

Thought Challenging: Now you're going to challenge those thoughts. How likely is it that your friend would really give up 10 years of good times because you called them late? How many times have they said they'd call and not called *you*? Likewise, will your client really not understand if you answer them tomorrow? Especially as it's after work hours? And even if they did leave you – do you *absolutely need* that client?

Remember that 80/20 thing? Maybe this client is one of those 80% you don't really need...

Hypothesis Testing: Now it's time to try and see whether your ruminations are justified or not for real. This process is called hypothesis testing and what it essentially involves is just testing what happens when you throw caution to the wind.

So take a smaller client and *try* not answering that e-mail... what happens? Likewise, *try* telling your friend you'll call them tomorrow. Or try not telling them at all.

The more you do this, the more comfortable you'll get with putting yourself and your energy levels first occasionally. And when you get to this point, you'll be much more able to switch off when you need to give yourself an hour break.

Cognitive behavioral therapy is also about learning useful 'tools' that you can use to maintain healthy thought processes. One example is to give yourself a time limit. If you struggle to let yourself unwind then try making a pact with yourself that you're going to take a time out just for 20 minutes.

What could happen that would be that bad in 20 minutes? Set an alarm on your phone and for those 20 minutes don't let *anything* else distract you.

Cognitive behavioral therapy gets a lot more in-depth and involved than that but the great thing about it is that you can do it anywhere and you don't even need to see a therapist in person. If you're regularly struggling with burnout try these tips. If you need *more* then consider booking yourself in to see a professional cognitive behavioral therapist. They can genuinely change your life.

NUTRITION, EXERCISE AND SLEEP

Now you've got your 'mental game' down you just need to think about looking after yourself.

We've discussed how your energy levels are finite, how you can burnout your adrenal glands and how you psychologically need time off. This is true for *everyone*.

Where we vary though, is in how much we can do before we end up collapsing. This is largely a matter of our health.

Don't you just hate those people who seem like they have boundless energy? They tend to have ripped abs, they always have their shirts off, their teeth are shiny white and they have amazing lives where they earn tons of money, travel the world, constantly are doing new things with friends and always seem happy.

Don't you wish you could take a leaf out of their book?

The trick is just to make sure you're looking after yourself and giving yourself the nutrition, sleep and exercise you need.

This is hard when you're burned out so it's something of a vicious cycle/catch 22. By applying the rules above though and making subtle changes though you can make a gradual difference over time leading to a full transformation.

Diet

The best diet in terms of avoiding burnout is one that is filled with natural, nutrient rich foods. That means you want to avoid useless empty carbs (cake, sweets and soda drinks) which cause a sugar spike followed by a crash and you want to avoid overly processed food that's had all the goodness removed from it (takeaways and ready meals).

Instead, you want to eat complex carbs (things like sweet potatoes and vegetables) for steady energy, you want to get fats for energy, absorption and testosterone (especially for guys) and you want to get protein which provides your body with the building blocks it needs to create muscle and more importantly – your neurotransmitters. (And don't forget fiber too which will keep your systems running smoothly)

Why is protein so important? Because it's packed with amino acids like L- tyrosine, phenylalanine and L-theanine. What you need to know about these particular amino acids is that they form the building blocks of our neurotransmitters. Thus they can help you to avoid adrenal fatigue. At the same time, they can also help you to produce more serotonin which will keep your neurochemistry nicely in balance. Certain vitamins and minerals do this too such as vitamin B6. Make sure you eat plenty of red meat (particularly organic meat and grass fed beef) and that you consume fruit and vegetables. Don't worry about the sugar from the fruit and veg, eating nutrient dense food will speed up your metabolism and keep you fuller so you'll lose weight in other places.

Red meats also have the benefit of containing things like creatine and CoQ10. These are supplements used by real athletes in order to improve the energy efficiency of their mitochondria. Mitochondria are little 'energy plants' that live in our cells and that convert glucose into ATP (adenosine triphosphate) AKA useable energy.

Oh and drink *plenty* of water.

Sleep

One of the best ways to recover from physical *or* mental stress is to get lots of sleep. You probably already knew this but are you doing the necessary work to ensure that your sleep is the best quality it can be? Sleep should be an absolute priority for everyone interested in optimal health and performance so make sure it is for you to.

A few simple changes:

- Make sure you are getting enough sleep (8 hours)
- Make your room completely dark and silent as far as possible
- Take a warm bath or shower before bed
- Avoid looking at bright screens right before bed
- Try to maintain a regular schedule

Exercise

Exercise helps your body to become far more energy efficient, it elevates your mood and it improves your sleep. As mentioned, something simple like a walk in the park can actually be sufficient to result in significant benefits.

But better than that would be to engage in what is known as 'HIIT' training. This is 'High Intensity Interval Training' and it involves alternating bursts of 70-100% effort with periods of light 'active recovery'. For instance then, you might sprint for 1 minute and then jog lightly for 3 and repeat.

This form of exercise results in the fastest weight loss with the minimal effort. What's more, it also has been shown to result in the creation of more mitochondria – to a greater extent than other forms of exercise.

RECOVERING FROM BURNOUT

All the previous advice can help you to avoid burnout and what's more, it will also give you the tools you need to get burnout under control if it has already occurred.

Sometimes though, you'll find that everything has gotten on top of you to the point where you can't see the light at the end of the tunnel. At this point, making incremental changes to your lifestyle and time management strategies isn't going to be enough.

In this case, what can you do?

HOW TO RECOVER FROM BURNOUT

The most obvious way to help yourself recover from burnout is to schedule some time off from your work or whatever else it is that is causing you stress. Going on holiday abroad and staying somewhere hot and sunny can be a great tonic but bear in mind that the act of going on holiday itself can be stressful (because of packing as well as the fact that you'll have a mountain of work waiting for you upon your return).

In some cases then it might make more sense to holiday locally. Book yourself a long weekend and stay in a spa where you can get various treatments and completely relax your mind.

Another important step to take is to remove the primary stressors that have led you to this point. Taking time off will allow your body to recover and you can use the burnout prevention techniques to ensure that the problem doesn't come back. But if the issue is something more pressing like a troubled relationship, like a bad job or like an illness, then you should also focus on trying to solve that issue. Sometimes this won't be possible but in the face of severe, acute and ongoing workplace stress for instance you should at least consider looking into changing your job. Remember, you don't actually have to *leave* your job with nothing lined up – just try looking at other potential career options in your spare time in case something comes up. The best way to tackle stress and thus to give yourself more mental energy, is to identify an ongoing stressor and then eliminate it.

Alternatively, instead of taking time out, you might decide to dedicate a whole day simply to having a 'refresh'. This means taking some time out to try and address smaller stressors and to make life easier for yourself where possible.

Maybe you'll tidy the house and throw out things you don't need, maybe you'll get a new computer, maybe you'll stock up on food or maybe you'll take time out of your normal schedule in order to catch up on all your correspondence. While these might seem like small, simple things; they will combine to give you the feeling of being 'on top' of everything which means just a little less to take up your mental energy going forward. As a result you'll be more resilient to stress and much less likely to suffer burnout. Sometimes you just have to hit the 'reset button' and while you're at it you might want to get a new haircut or outfit as a visual reminder of your new lease on life and new attitude.

Learning from the Experience

While you want to rid yourself from burnout as quickly as possible to protect your health and to get yourself in a productive and happy state of mind again, this doesn't mean that you should dismiss it entirely. Every case of burnout should be viewed as a learning experience.

As we've mentioned previously in this book, burnout and the ways we cope with burnout involve a lot of individual differences. Among other things this means that the triggers will vary from person to person, as will the amount that we can 'take' before collapsing.

When you burn out, try to make a note of what it was that caused it and why it happened. By knowing what the triggers were, you'll be well equipped to prevent yourself from getting into the same situation again in the future. Likewise, make note of what it was that helped you to feel better again. The more data you collect the better able you will be to keep yourself performing optimally and avoid failure.

CONCLUSION

So there you have it: everything you could possibly need to know about burnout. Now you know what it actually *is* in terms of your neurochemistry, you know what the causes are and you know how to prevent it from happening and to treat it when it occurs.

Using this information, you can now follow a simple plan to avoid burnout and to make sure that you're able to keep operating optimally.

Here's the simple plan that you need to execute:

#1 Hit Reset

If you're feeling stressed and close to burnout already then you need to hit the rest button. That means taking some time off and recuperating while also using the time to get your life organized, to assess yourself (like a 'crash report' almost) and to look at whether there are any big stressors in your life you can eliminate.

#2 Make More Time

Next you need to think about that 'energy management' thing we covered. That means making sure that you aren't cramming too much into your day even if you *can* afford the time. Outsource and delegate the tasks that you don't have time for yourself and that don't require you to be personally overseeing them. Likewise, be sure to occasionally say no to invitations and cancel anything you really don't have time for.

#3 Learn How to Relax

Learn how to relax mentally and physically and schedule this into your routine. That might mean using CBT in order to get yourself mentally to switch off or it might just mean spending time doing things you love and that completely engage your mind so that you aren't stressing about other matters. Spend at least an hour a day *actively* switching off from the world (this means not taking on anyone else's problems too) and remember to prioritize this recovery ahead of 'answering another e-mail'. We all know that they never end...

#4 Improve Your Lifestyle

Getting outside will give you more vitamin D and fresh air to help you sleep better and improve your energy levels. Exercising will give you more energy and increase your mitochondria – especially if you use HIIT. Make sure you eat a mineral and vitamin dense diet, avoid simple carbs and prioritize your sleep. Look after yourself – even if it takes time – and ultimately you will be able to do more without burning out as fast.